The Vampire Seducer

John Danen

Published by John Danen, 2023.

THE VAMPIRE SEDUCER

First edition. August 18, 2023.

ISBN: 979-8224457793

Written by John Danen.

Table of Contents

To all the night hunters

Introduction.

I am doing this book because I have realized that there are enormous similarities between the vampire and the seducer. The vampire is dedicated to evil, a being of darkness corrupted by evil. It is a nocturnal being with great capacities for seduction, enormous power, and long life.

The seducer is another being of darkness as well, with great capacities for seduction, although not innate but worked on in a very laborious way. He also has enormous power and long life in seduction, and if the facet of "dark seduction" predominates the seducer will be dedicated to evil, so they are very similar in terms of what they are each.

The vampire bites and gives eternal life to the one he bites, or kills directly. The seducer conquers the girls, kisses them and this is the equivalent of the vampire's bite. Then he gives them a good or bad life according to what they deserve, usually a bad but bearable one. The only important difference is that the vampire is a supernatural being and the seducer has almost supernatural abilities too, but he is not. The essence is very similar.

I hope you don't take this book as a joke, because what I'm about to write is of great importance and I'm sure you didn't realize it. Ah! and if there are real vampires, they better not come to visit me, and if they do, they better offer something of quality, like eternal life and things like that, otherwise, I'm very happy to be a seducer.

The vampire's clothing.

The vampire is much more elegant than the seducer without any doubt. The classic vampire of the nineteenth century wears a cape, high hat, elegant suit, high collar, white, red and black colors and has a refinement and an elegant demeanor, largely contributed by the clothing. The romantic vampire, that is to say of the nineteenth century, is very well dressed with clothes of the highest quality, and often wears attire that are no longer fashionable today, such as the cape or the cane.

The vampire attracts attention wherever he goes. He also wears dark sunglasses, preferably blue, with them he is able to go out in the daylight. Not everyone can, but some can.

The seducer's attire.

If the seducer does not belong to the "school of bearing" that I explained in the book Seduction 5.0, he does not dress excessively well, he dresses casually, as he pleases, he can be elegant, he can be sporty, in short, he creates his own style and identifies himself with that style. The seducer never dresses as elegantly and well as a vampire, because his refinement and exquisiteness is not as much. Only some very, very fine seducers come close to the very high quality of the vampire's clothing and elegance.

Command staff.

One accessory that vampires often carry is their staff. You probably haven't realized what this cane means. This cane is carried by the vampire not because he is old or it is difficult for him to walk. It is the baton of command, the one carried by kings, princes, people of high nobility, or military, chieftains, or dictators. Carrying the baton means that you have authority. It means that the one who carries it is the one who commands. The baton gives you a status above all others, you will be the one who commands and directs everyone. Dracula and many vampires carry it. This is an elegant, lavishly crafted and ornate staff, made of precious metals and stones, and gives the vampire a wealthy and powerful touch. Usually the vampire belongs to nobility or even royalty and that is why he has it.

The baton of command is held by authorities, mayors, marshals, emperors, presidents of countries and of course... vampires.

You can also defend yourself with it if necessary, giving strong blows to the enemies.

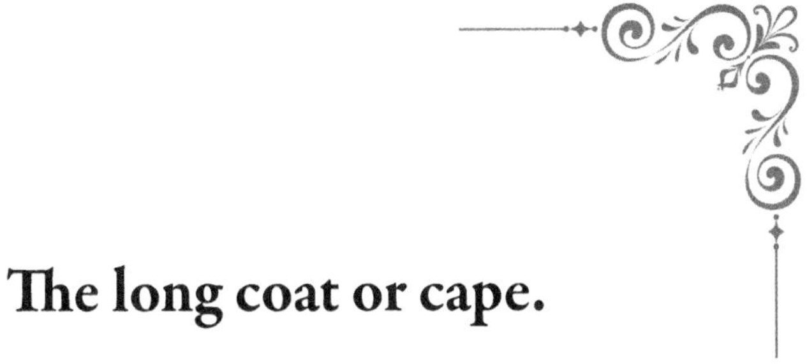

The long coat or cape.

That's right, all vampires are dressed in capes or long coats. They are garments that give the mysterious touch because they almost completely hide the body. From there they can draw weapons or wrap the victims with it. The vampire can move his cloak and disappear inside it away from enemies. A vampire without his cloak is not fully vampire. This cloak gives you the elegant and distinguished touch. If it is black on the outside and red on the inside with a high collar, all the better. Today the vampire can wear a long coat with a high collar as a cape. Its function is the same and does not clash in these times. The coat will always be made of fine silk on the inside. With this coat or cloak you wrap the girls and you have them totally in your power.

Rings.

The vampire will always wear an exaggerated amount of rings with gigantic stones of all colors. This will give you the opulent, sophisticated and exquisite touch. A touch that sets you apart from other mortals, never better said. The vampire's jewelry box must be very wealthy because they are really precious stones of high value and enormous size that must cost a lot. The vampire usually acquires his rings as part of the heritage of his ancestral family, and they serve to fascinate women, because he is more ornamented than them, but much more. The vampire has a high knowledge of goldsmithing and jewelry, and greatly values these rings, otherwise it is not explained that he always wears those gigantic rings.

Bracelets.

The vampire will also wear solid gold bracelets, never silver because they bother his eyes. As I said before, the vampire's jewelry box will be full of money if he has not killed him before, because all this must cost a lot of money, plus they are old pieces that go back several generations and are often inherited. If the vampire has economic problems it would be enough to sell some of these pieces and he could live a whole year, but he will never get rid of anything because they have an immense value for him.

Most likely, the bracelet is engraved with the initials of a centuries-old love. The vampire is a romantic at heart, and in this he differs significantly from the seducers, who are not romantic at all.

Pendants and brooches.

The vampire also usually wears pendants, but never with a cross, but can wear the order of the dragon, or some insignia, or ancient military distinction. It will always be even a gigantic brooch, which confers the status of general of armies, or leader of large territories.

The mortal who sees this does not know the enormous importance of these jewels, and is simply amazed to see the elaboration and ornamentation of these brooches and pendants. For the vampire they are very precious things and he never gets rid of them. Most of them are centuries old.

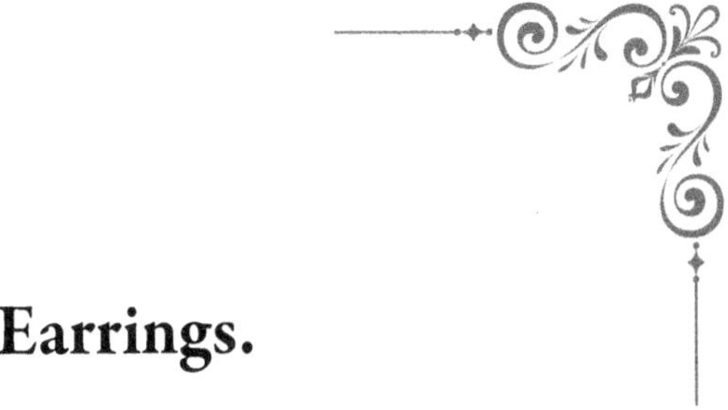

Earrings.

The vampire does not usually wear earrings, perhaps some more modernized vampires may wear them, but in general they do not wear them. The seducer may wear them. But it is rather an occasional thing in both, the vast majority of vampires and seducers do not wear earrings.

Hats.

The vampire will wear a long hat, preferably black. The hat gives distinction and elegance and differentiates him from the common people who do not wear it. The hat will always be a top hat. This hat gives the touch of the elegant and refined nineteenth century and the superior status that corresponds to it by lineage, possessions, or titles. I will talk more about how to incorporate all these clothes and accessories to the seducer's attire.

Watches.

The vampire seducer is a huge fan of watches and will have them in all colors, preferably blue and black, also red. A good vampire seducer has a minimum of six watches. He also has pocket watches that he displays at night in pubs when he is seducing a woman, which gives him the very elegant touch that only the vampire seducer has. The seductive vampire makes the accessories a part of himself and these give him more elegance, glamour and sophistication. Of course he will never wear any digital watch, everything will always be analog and with clear numbers, very large Arabic numerals. It is especially valued a watch with white background with black Arabic numerals very visible.

When he is in the pub with the girl he looks at his pocket watch and the girl will be impressed by such sophistication and opulence.

Coat of arms.

The seductive vampire who has prospered and has become an opulent rich man will seek to buy a house with a coat of arms to give himself more haughty and noble airs. This large and solemn old house may well be the dwelling, at least temporarily, of the seducer. If this seducer does not come from the nobility, the action he will take will be to buy or build himself a house with a coat of arms. If the house does not have one, he can design his own coat of arms and have it carved on the front of his new mansion. Any stonemason will be able to do it easily and you will have your coat of arms.

A seductive vampire must differentiate himself with all these pompous and bombastic things from all the other people in the populace.

Vampires.

Just as there are seductive vampires, there are also women totally similar to us, the vampires. The difference between the vampire and the vampires is that the vampires have a totally easy life, even gifted. Every night they go out hunting and they hunt in abundance and really this is very satisfying for them, but it has no merit. Because the striker who scores goals is better than the goalkeeper who allows himself to score them, for them the pressure is constant to get them and they have to select. We are the ones who push for this to happen, so these vampires although some may be attractive, the vampire himself despises them deeply and repudiates them. We don't boost the ego of these egomaniacs anymore.

General appearance of the vampire.

In general the vampire looks magnificent, he is young and attractive many times, other times he is middle-aged with a little gray hair, and these give him even more attractive. He wears expensive and sophisticated elegant clothes, has fine and elegant gestures, knows history. Another characteristic of the vampire is that he is a man of deep sensitivity, lover of all kinds of arts. He is a sybarite of clothing and is also an exquisite seducer who will undermine the resistance of his victims with his charm and his foreign-accented language. The vampire speaks finely, tells wonderful stories of distant worlds that only he knows. The vampire enraptures the girls with his refinement and imperial bearing. The vampire knows about history, geography, science, politics and the dark arts. He has spent hundreds of years learning things and refining his customs. The vampire is a well of wisdom and the materialization of supreme elegance.

Vampire aged due to not drinking enough blood

Vampire full of power.

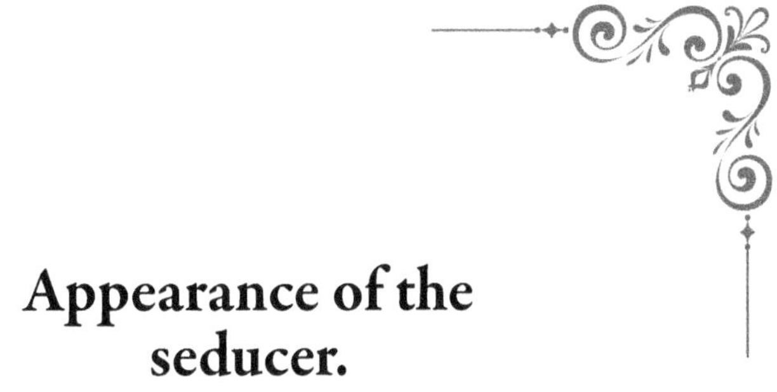

Appearance of the seducer.

The seducer will be rather less elegant than the vampire, he usually wears many accessories like the vampire, such as rings, earrings, bracelets, pendants. He wears elegant clothes if he feels like it. The seducer may also have fine gestures, but he will not reach the extreme sophistication, elegance and refinement that a true vampire has. The seducer will age much worse than the vampire because he is not immortal, so he will try to compensate this loss of beauty with a greater number of complements and better clothes. In any case, the seducer will almost always look excellent, not magnificent like the vampire, but very attractive.

If the seducer wants to look as elegant as him, what he has to do is to copy his clothes in a disguised way, instead of a cape he will wear a long coat, instead of a brooch a pin or a badge, he can also raise the collar of his shirt like a vampire. Imitate colors and walk with distinguished airs. Speak slowly, pausing, look at people and transmit with your eyes the essence of your stories. The look is the most important weapon of both.

The seducer can and should incorporate the essence of the vampire into his clothing and behavior. Both appear beautiful on the outside but are monsters on the inside. Seducers are nothing more than vampires who have not realized they are vampires.

Horror story.

In a lush forest beyond the Carpathian Mountains, there once existed a castle where a man named Vlad Tepes, alias "the Impaler" actually lived. It is said that this man impaled his victims who were usually Muslim prisoners of war and then ate while watching them writhe and agonize nailed to stakes. He also impaled quite a respectable sum, some 10,000 impaled. It is also said that Transylvania was the birthplace of Count St. Germain himself, the immortal who astonished many of the courts of the 18th century, especially the French.

It was said that this man never ate, that he knew how to transmute lead into gold, that he spoke eight languages, that he had lived in the time of Jesus Christ, that he could play many instruments. He knew all sciences and was charming. He was an immortal man who reappeared in the nineteenth and twentieth centuries and is still seen today, maybe it is true that vampires exist, I really believe they do.

By some mysterious mechanism it may happen that a man discovers something through alchemy, or it may simply happen that a biological oddity appears that perpetuates and reproduces itself. With blood, with some elixir of eternal youth, with the philosopher's stone, or however it happens, the vampire became immortal.

And here in Galicia there was also a man, he did not live in a castle, he was not called Vlad, but the nickname could also be "the impaler" because he impaled them with his thick member. Another similarity between seducers and vampires, we are both impalers.

Vampires make men and women suffer, seducers make women enjoy, especially when they are impaled.

Music and Rocanrol.

They both like rock and roll, the vampire without any doubt must listen to metal, heavy and industrial music, also church organ music and classical music; because he is a person of fine manners and very sophisticated tastes. The vampire with a tendency to romanticism will be able to listen to some softer music, also classical, in this case violins. Symphony orchestras will be well known and valued by the vampire and I would wager that he likes Vivaldi. What I am sure of is that the vampire loves Bach. Where the vampire is most at home is listening to church organ music, so Bach is certainly his favorite composer. About the music that exists right now we could say that the vampire likes evil bands so to speak, dark, gothic, or techno metal bands with heavy, rock and industrial sounds.

Musicians and bands that the vampire is certain to like are as follows:

- Marilyn Manson.
- Rammstein.
- Einsbrecher.
- Blutengel which is a very vampiric group.
- Sopor Aeternus. Vampiric to the maximum.

The seducer if in him dominates the dark side, that is to say if he is a "Dark seducer" will have exactly the same tastes, liking the organ music and these groups before, but if he dominates his facet of light, then he will have other different tastes and other groups as for example:

- Moby.
- Mike Oldfield.
- Killer swing.
- Illegals.
- Roxy Music.
- Omd.

The former are groups of darkness and the latter of light.

As the most vampiric song in the world I consider "Death soulds" by Sopor Aeternus. An excellent music that speaks precisely about vampires.

Seductive vampire rocker.

Absinthe.

As the vampire said in the movie to his beautiful lady.
"Absinthe is the aphrodisiac of the self,
the green fairy wants your soul
But rest assured with me you are safe."

And so it is, vampires drink absinthe and so do half-crazed seducers like me.

With this drink you go out of your mind, you have enormous creativity and you visualize everything much better, you really go out of your mind with the green fairy. Yet another similarity between vampires and seducers. Dracula himself drank it in the 19th century.

Mantra.

Repeat after me.

-I want to

I wish to

I decree

I demand

May all my wishes materialize into reality, for the fucking power is with me.

And I shout this loud and strong without fear of being heard, without caring what others think, I am one with the fucking power and nothing bad can happen to me.

Thanks to fucking power I materialize everything I desire and this is the source of my power. My ability to visualize and the absolute belief that fucking power provides me with everything I want, truly empowers me.

Beyond time and space, crossing oceans and mountain ranges, the fucking power brings me what I ask for. A mystical revelation, a flowing river, the sea breaking against the rocks, the cloud that covers the sun, everything is part of the fucking Power, I absorb it, I impregnate it with my thought and emit it and it returns to me with what I desire.

God does not play dice.

Everything that happens to you, even if it seems to be very bad, you must accept it, because you do not really know what the consequences of what you desire will be. But God, who is on high and sees all things and knows all things, knows what is good for you and therefore does not grant it to you. He takes away what you want because he has a better plan for you, so do not regret anything, God does not play dice, do not be discouraged if things do not work out, it is all part of the plan and so it should be and it is perfect.

In the universe it has been discovered that there is a super symmetry that has no logic and is the proof that this is something very big, or an infinitely powerful simulation, or a work of someone or something with its immutable laws. Among these laws is that you can attract what you desire by visualizing it and God wants it and is pleased.

Einstein, one of the most intelligent men in the world said "God does not play dice", accept and be grateful for what God gives you.

Nocturnality.

The seducer and the vampire are both creatures of the night, the true seducer denies the sun and only comes out to fulfill his function at nightfall, exactly as the vampire does. This is another great similarity that has led me to establish links between the two. The seducer develops his predation in the dark almost always, even more if he is a dark seducer, then he will avoid the light as a vampire and during the day he will only sleep, if he can afford it. He will only go out to do the minimum shopping, always dressed with a lot of sun protection, wearing sunglasses that take away the sunlight that bothers and harms him so much. It does not harm him as much as the vampire, but enough. The seducer will never practice the "daygame" which is called by him "diegame", because it is something that almost kills him and causes him strong aversion.

The night is our friend, it camouflages the defects that you are having with age, you do not notice so much the lack of hair, or wrinkles, not even if you are a little overweight, you notice this as clearly as in the light of day. The night is favorable, because the darkness beautifies our body, camouflages our defects. In addition, the alcohol that they drink by themselves weakens them and makes them more receptive to our charms.

True hunters are always nocturnal, they lurk in the dark. The vampire is full at night, the seducer the same. The night is magic, the night is our life. The seducer and the vampire gather at dawn with the satisfaction of duty done. Sometimes they return to their lair alone, sometimes accompanied by new and stupendous girls who come to enjoy the pleasures of the dark side that same night. Some of them will become vampires, in this case good ones, while others will become staunch followers of the seducer. From good comes evil and from evil comes good.

Taste for risk.

The seducer and the vampire love the risk, they could each be at home, one in his castle and the other in his apartment with a nice and hot woman. The vampire would have his vampiress and would be happy and the seducer would have his girlfriend and they wouldn't look for anything else, but what they both like the most is to go hunting. Sometimes the prey lasts a night or a few days, and as soon as the piece is acquired, it is eliminated from their lives. Sometimes not, other times because of the quality and excellent behavior of the woman, they are turned into vampires or our most fervent acolytes, our intimate friends who forgive us everything, adore us and value us very much. Our triad, the three women that every good seducer hoards for his enjoyment. This triad also appears in the movie "Dracula" by Francis Ford Coppola. Dracula had his triad, three wonderful women who were in his castle, and so he spent the centuries consoling himself for not having his true beloved Elizabetha. With this triad Dracula was much happier than in solitude and immortality was more bearable for him.

We, like the vampire, also form our triads or quartets and console ourselves with these women when the hunt is not satisfactory.

And what do I think about flirting, flirting is something with a lot of risk, even more than climbing, but the risk is where you really feel alive.

Creation of the group of acolytes.

Dracula has servants, rather slaves, to whom he gives part of his powers and they protect him during the day and serve him faithfully. These acolytes, these servants, like Renfield, are valued and appreciated by the vampire although he treats them rather badly.

We seducers do not have such clearly helpful acolytes, but we do have our followers, our followers in social networks who consider us as someone very great and who defend and value us a lot. We dedicate ourselves to show them the dark side, to teach them the techniques of both the light and the dark, we dedicate ourselves to train them, to transfer our knowledge, and they are very grateful for it. We also have a similarity in this, besides we give our followers a much better treatment than the vampire gives them. Do not confuse followers with girls, acolytes are tough and shameless men.

The vampire's abode.

The vampire likes to live in a rickety castle in the mountains, a castle with super outdated, cold, damp and gloomy furnishings. A castle that he can't afford properly and that has a lot of dirt, cobwebs, and strange junk from centuries past abandoned gathering dust. This castle shows the grandeur and opulence of the Vapiric Count centuries ago, but today it is decrepit and overgrown. Dracula is not very aware of payments and is illuminated with candles in the old fashioned way, this gives the castle a dark and gloomy touch. He also has there his servants who serve him, his acolytes who protect him from the light. In his crypt Dracula is at ease resting without any disturbing light.

This castle is used to welcome visitors and impress them with the opulence and former splendor of the rooms, although in reality what it conveys is a very large abandonment and decline, but this is the way its owner likes it best, dilapidated and in frank decline, so the castle enjoys an excellent romantic and gloomy halo.

The abode of the seducer.

The seducer's abode is a much more modest house than the vampire's. The seducer likes to live up high, so he prefers penthouses and top floors where he can enjoy the view. The seducer likes to live up high, so he prefers penthouses and top floors from where he can enjoy the view. He takes his victims up there to enjoy the terrace if he has one, or at least to be up high and be able to see a lot of territory. If the house is in front of a forest, all the better.

The seducer is a music enthusiast, and in his house he will always have a high-powered musical equipment, with which he and his girls will listen to the great songs that he always has at high volume, and with it the girls will enjoy enormously.

The seducer, like the vampire, also plays an instrument, a bass, a guitar, often a musical organ with a high level of mastery.

Customs.

The vampire rises at dusk and goes out all night in search of new victims. The night is all magic and there in the darkness, always lurking, hides the vampire ready to bite. We seducers are like vampires and we also go out at night, during the day we are resting, dozing and resting, to be fully operational at sunset.

Another habit is not to worry about anything and always be friendly and cheerful. What is there to worry about when you are aware that you are a seductive vampire? Nothing, you just take care of enjoying yourself.

Sadomaso.

Both the seducer and the vampire have their triad. These women are dependent and hallucinated with your enormous power, they live to serve you and give you pleasures. They are at your command, to what you order them, because they appreciate your qualities so much that they let themselves do in the sexual field what you want, that's why both the seducer and the vampire have at least a triad mounted.

These acolytes enjoy pleasing the master and do whatever you ask them to do.

And as there are differences between the master and the slaves, they obviously have to satisfy you and fulfill all your perversions, because they are very lucky to be with you and they should be grateful for it. Thus, both the seducer of the highest level who has become a slave master, and the vampire do sadomaso with their slaves.

Sadomaso Yeah!

Oral sex.

The vampire is a sexual sybarite very fond of oral sex, especially the one they give him.

A woman with lips painted in intense red emphasizes more this part of the body so fleshy, if we put a mask that covers almost all the face except the eyes and mouth, this will affect the morbid that gives that mouth, which will be another sexual organ and the vampire will enjoy watching how his slave fela.

This mask can be put on for that, to emphasize more the sexual function of the mouth and to dominate it. Any well-done fellatio must be perfectly seen by the vampire to be totally satisfactory. The vampire will become very demanding in this field and will not compromise the slightest failure.

Favorite cities and places.

The vampire and the seducer like the same things. Leaving aside the moment of seduction when you have to go to the pub and there is no other choice, we will go to almost the same places. The pub is so to speak our natural environment, the darkness, being camouflaged among the people is a joy. But really the place where both the seducer and the vampire are comfortable in their time of rest from predation, is in the forest, the mountains, and the rivers.

Everyone likes to go to the beach and that's fine too, I'm not saying it's not good, but it is preferable for my taste the high mountains with large forests and mighty rivers, where you can jump from the trees to the river and enjoy the current. Besides these places are much less visited than the beaches, which are totally saturated. Here you find the relaxation and peace that nature gives you, and you feel great.

Think a little, Dracula's dwelling was not in a city, it was lost in the mountains of Transylvania, as the seducer the same, he usually has a house on the outskirts of the city, in the middle of nature, then he always goes out at night to hunt, and at dawn he hides again in his dark abode. My house is like this, it is on the outskirts of the city and overlooks a forest, it is also shady because it faces north and I never get the sun, so more points for my belief that if I'm not a vampire, at least I have enough to do with them.

At night I leave the window open and listen to the owls in the forest hooting. The forest is right in front of me and occupies the entire expanse of the view. The owls hoot with their super pleasant night song, and I hear them from the bed. Many times I lean out the window and listen to them intently, sometimes I'm tempted to go down into the woods at night and just be there listening to the creatures. I think I will do that very soon.

Also near me there is another even deeper forest which I have called "the fragrant and shady forest" like the song of the illegals. There I go to do meditation, I have even seen huge eagles. The eagles fly away as soon as they see me because even the biggest predator, when it sees the vampire, flees. In that fragrant and shady forest is fucking great, you feel in communion with nature and use those energies to visualize better and relax, and so you use the fucking power more easily.

Medieval cities that have areas classified as historical, the so-called "old cities" have much more charm. These old towns are the place where the vampire likes to live, and so does the seducer. There are old stone and wood pubs located in these "old areas" that were stables a hundred years ago and that is where the seducer feels at ease, as they remind him of the vampire's castle.

We are not so fond of modern pubs, as they are not sophisticated in furniture, rather minimalist. It is the archaic pubs full of wood, stone and rock or even Celtic music that excite us.

Here in my Santiago de Compostela I enjoy countless gloomy and gloomy pubs where I take refuge like a vampire. The rainier and less sunny the city the better, because it hurts the vampire and also the nocturnal seducer who has little tolerance for the sun and always wants to be in the shade. So Santiago de Compostela is a good city, both for a vampire and for a seducer, because it is always cloudy and raining and the sun does not harm us. Those of us who are used to going out at night the day dazzles us with so much light.

Other recommended cities are Segovia, Oviedo, Santander and Castro Urdiales in Cantabria.

I always go to rivers because there you are in the shade of the trees and the sun doesn't bother you. So many similarities between seducers and vampires! The old cities, the rainy weather and the dark stone pubs.

Bach, Vivaldi,
recommended pieces and
instruments.

The seductive vampire will listen to classical music, especially baroque music. The greatest exponents are Vivaldi and Bach. Vivaldi has a wide variety of quality music, lots of wonderful pieces where violins and mandolins are predominant. Bach focuses more on the organ, cantatas and oboes. Especially interesting is the church organ music. This music is mechanical, cold, artificial, and creates a magical atmosphere. If you listen to the cathedral organ it will leave your skin crawling, as it really is something sublime and grandiose. Cathedral organ music is the best music that can exist, above the classical violin music because it tends to be a bit pompous.

Another magical instrument is the harpsichord, which is a solemn and mechanical antique piano that gives an exquisite and elegant touch to music. Here I include Handel as well who is an accomplished harpsichordist who faced off against Maestro Scarlatti, the other master of this instrument in an epic duel.

I am going to put a selection of the best musical pieces that every seductive vampire should listen to while he is at home keeping vigil, ready to go out to prey. Buxtehude is another composer who also deserves to be heard.

I like rock and I guess you do too, but take my advice and listen to these pieces at high volume, they are a blast.

Bach:

Bwv 593 Organ Concerto in A Minor by Bach. I especially recommend this one.

Fugue in G-minor BWV 578 - J S Bach

Bach - Fantasia and fugue in G minor BWV 542

Bach Prelude and fugue in B minor BWV 544

Bach Harpsichord Concerto No. 1 in_D_Min

BWV 593 Organ Concerto in A Minor. Highly recommended.

J S Bach Cantata BWV 29

Johann Sebastian Bach - Toccata and Fugue in D minor BWV 565. The best known.

Vivaldi:

Vivaldi Concerto for Violin and Organ

Antonio Vivaldi La tempesta di mare.

Gloria in excelsis deo. Antonio Vivaldi

Vivaldi,_Concerto_for_2_mandolins

Vivaldi RV 230 C for organ. How well the bastard Vivaldi did it! on a par with the master Bach.

Vivaldi Symphony in C Major Allegro. Of violins, excellent

Antonio Vivaldi La tempesta di mare. Another one for violins

Buxtehude:

Dietrich_Buxtehude,_Toccata_en_Fa_majeur.

Alleluia Buxtehude

Handel:

Handel harpsichord Suite No. 7 in G min

The night.

The night is magic, at night everything takes on a darker aspect, people are afraid because they do not look good, it is easier to hide, the night camouflages your defects, your centenary vampire wrinkles, at night everything is made up. Besides, in the night party people are happy, they drink, laugh and dance, the festive atmosphere predisposes to love and passion. It is an open market with lots of interactions. If you are really committed to your seductive mission, there are so many, many possibilities, it's a real feast. It's really this night market where the most fluid and heated exchanges occur. Many times girls do things at night that they surprise themselves the next day and don't even dare to remember.

We take advantage of all this, the night is not our mission, it is part of us. We go out when it gets dark and come back when it gets light. We are truly night vampires.

At night
Under the full moon
At about twelve o'clock
The vampire leaves
To procure other enjoyment
The dark pub
The right place
To deploy hard
Amassed power
And as a consequence

 JOHN DANEN

From his excellent work
Get a pretty girl
And the enjoyment proceeds
All night long.

Loneliness.

The vampire is a solitary being, and does not like the company of others very much. He goes to the lonely beach, to the lonely river, to the lonely mountains, all alone. It is only when he wants to interact with women that he lets himself be seen in crowded places. Places that he does not really like excessively, but which are necessary. Parties or sunny terraced areas.

Where he is comfortable is in the darkness of the pub.

The initiatory lake of the vampire.

The vampire in the darkness of his abode plans his journeys through unknown and wild lands. He always travels alone on these voyages of exploration and initiation. Then, once he has investigated the terrain, he can take there his multiple and valuable women who will enjoy it twice as much. They will enjoy the place without having to investigate anything, you give them everything already done, and, of course, they also enjoy the vampire fucker himself.

The vampire does not usually travel to cities, but to inhospitable places in the middle of nature, there at night he recharges his energies by absorbing the power of that place.

Rivers, lakes, reservoirs, or any freshwater stream are the vampire's favorite place.

He will travel hundreds of miles to find the right place. His new place of power.

Once in the place of power, the vampire will walk all the paths, bathe in all the rivers, explore all the forests. The vampire will bathe naked at sunset in the lake and will go out of his mind from so much enjoyment and pleasure.

There in solitude, lost in the woods, half-naked and far from civilization, he will have the revelations that will give him the power, to later, magnificently seduce almost all the girls that the vampire wishes to seduce.

In the dark night, while it rains lightly, the vampire dives deep into the lake beyond the mountains. The full moon shines in the firmament and the stars tinge the surface of the lake with twinkling light.

In the depths of the lake, without any light, in total darkness, completely sunk to the bottom, the vampire remains there holding his breath as long as possible, until he can no longer hold it, and symbolically dies.

Then the uprising takes place.

The vampire emerges from the depths of the lake, naked, with nothing, totally reduced to his belongings, but, from that moment of death and resurrection, the only thing he will do will be to acquire more and more fucking power. From the depths of the lake in the starry night, the vampire emerges transformed into a new self, even more powerful than the previous one.

The vampire's lake is extensive and surrounded by large forests, where he goes for his metamorphosis, his death and resurrection, to emerge all the fears and insecurities of the vampire are left in the lake and he comes out clean, pure and powerful.

From the darkness of a lake lost in the mountains, the light that will irremediably trap the women who interact with the vampire will emerge.

This is a ritual, an empowering act.

Out of darkness comes light.

The moon.

The vampire climbs the highest mountain he can find and there at the top looks up at the moon. He always carries his magic items that are charged there.

This is another good place to acquire power. The viewpoint of the mountain. There alone at night you absorb more and more celestial and telluric power, which is then transformed into pure fucking power, which allows you to get everything you want. A well performed visualization in this place is much more easily transformed into pure reality. Sometimes just as it was imagined.

This power absorbed from nature, from the sky, and from the earth, is then stored and used at will by the vampire in the pub. His hunting ground.

From fear and death comes confidence and life.

Where there was nothing, a crowd appears.

From scarcity, abundance is created.

From loneliness, companionship emerges.

The reborn is here to claim yet another massacre.

The hot springs.

The vampire also bathes in hot springs that spring up on the banks of rivers. There, in these small pools, he not only enjoys and relaxes, but since they are quite crowded places, he socializes and many times, showing off his powerful charisma, he flirts there with big-assed girls who have either been selected by the seductive vampire, or who have been attracted by his imposing figure. Of course, one must avoid very sunny days, because the sun bothers the vampire enormously, preferring cloudy days, sunsets, or even nights.

The vampire goes to the bathtub with his bottle of champagne and his beautiful girlfriend to have a great sex session that will end in only one possible way. The vampire certainly ends up fucking the woman who is with him in the bathtub. A woman who has become hotter than the bath itself while having sex with the vampire and must be satiated with an excellent vampiric and lustful sex.

Vampire culture.

The vampire is a well of wisdom. He absorbs everything, he investigates, he delves deep. The vampire is extremely interested in all kinds of matters, especially those that have to do with antiquity and the lavish mansions that were there. The Romans and their architecture and engineering excite the vampire.

The vampire knows about empires, knows perfectly the fall of Rome, the Holy Roman Empire, the conquests of Napoleon, the deeds of the Spanish Empire, the great battles, the great discoverers, the adventurers, the mystics.

He studies in depth legendary characters such as Casanova or Count Sant Germain. The vampire knows practically everything, he is also well versed in occult sciences, magic, mental power, quantum physics. The vampire believes in reincarnation, knows about music, plays the organ, learns from the great generals and architects, investigates mysterious events, occult energies. The vampire is an initiate, a teacher and a mystic, as well as an enormous seducer.

The magician.

The seductive vampire has knowledge of magic, is fascinated by the occult sciences, and investigates mythical historical figures such as the magician Merlin or Count Saint Germain. I am going to talk a little about this count who is a person who was probably a real vampire because he lived for hundreds of years appearing here and there in the courts amazing everyone with his wisdom, his skill for languages, science, music. He was described as a man who knew everything and who never died. He attributed his longevity and good physical appearance to the very philosopher's stone that kept him young, this stone transformed metals into gold and also served to manufacture the elixir of eternal youth.

The vampire is a magician, a little initiate who knows some elementary concepts of magic and uses it also for seduction, yes, the JD method works, and everything works, because we are not really seducing, we are creating, we are doing magic. Natural magic.

Witches.

Believe it or not, witches do exist and you can see them on the street in quite abundance, and I would even say that I have fucked one of them. These women here in Galicia are women who practice natural magic, they are healers, they know the plants and their healing abilities, they have notions of magic and also an innate facility to connect with the other side. They are women that although the name is a little scary, they are actually very good and loving, another thing are the bad witches who cast evil spells to bend wills, that would be bad magic and that is not what good witches do. Formerly all these concepts of magic were known by the Celtic druids, these were healers, judges and people of maximum authority.

All this knowledge was lost in part with the Romanization, and was scattered in remote villages treasured by the misnamed witches. These witches were unjustly burned many times because everything that was not Catholicism was considered paganism and heresy. Therefore all this arcane and distant knowledge of the Celts has been transmitted to us through these medieval witches until today. Today we have managed to collect practically all the ancient wisdom that existed, and the magic, the spell and the good witchcraft of the witches and meigas such as the Galician witches and witches are still in force.

Another thing is the witches of Spanish America that have a very different origin, which comes from shamanism and nahuales and all that, and that has little to do with European witches. This is a much darker subject and is not what I am talking about.

In general good natural witchcraft is quite concentrated in wicca, but sometimes it has contaminations of satanic dye that have nothing to do with natural witchcraft and others with shamanism in its most evil variant, what I am talking about is good witchcraft that does good and that simply shapes your reality without ever twisting any will. You have to do a lot of research to find the right books that tell you about magic without contaminations like the ones he talked about here.

Witches are good, they're hot and they fuck well, fuck a witch! When you're a vampire you're not afraid of witches, you fuck them!

What does a real vampire seducer look like today?

A seductive vampire today looks very good, usually dressed quite smartly in a jacket, or suit sometimes, giving preference to the colors red and black of course.

The seductive vampire likes accessories, so he will wear sunglasses to protect himself from the hated sun, and this is perhaps the essential accessory to go out during the day and one of the most important along with carved rings, pompous necklaces, pendants, and some earrings that can also be worn. All of good quality, the clothes will be comfortable and elegant as well as quality, but not branded. The look the vampire conveys is a tough, handsome guy who likes himself.

Opulence.

The vampire seducer is a winner, he has managed to make a great living and get out of the conventional system of working for others, so he will have free time and money to enjoy his seductive-vampire misdeeds.

He will have a good car, a good house, money in the bank, freedom to do whatever he wants, creative ideas to put into practice, and exciting projects to carry out. You will eat little but tasty food in good restaurants, and you will travel everywhere for as long as you feel like it; even indefinitely. You can afford to travel all year round and still make money.

Enough of being poor and living miserably! the vampire is living great and enjoying the huge amounts of money he gets. All this was thought out and materialized, after a lot of intelligent and hard work to achieve it.

Freedom.

The seductive vampire has freed himself from the thing that produces the most limitations and slavery, which is having a girlfriend. If he goes with a girl it will be for a rather short time, involving himself rather little. What the seductive vampire values most is freedom, to be able to travel wherever he wants, to be able to go out without giving explanations, to do whatever he wants. This is better than money or anything else, because it allows you to be yourself and do what you want for once and for all in your life. It's about time!

The greatest slavery you will ever have in your life will be to have a serious relationship with a woman. Avoid it at all costs!

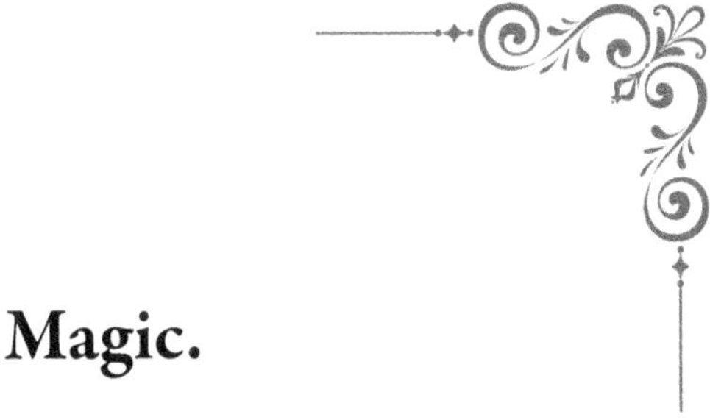

Magic.

Yes, the seductive vampire is really a magician who creates his reality with his thoughts. To materialize what you desire you have to imagine very clearly and then act as if you have already achieved it. Ask and it will be given to you, you can read Paracelsus, empower your powers with the crystal ball. Practice the art of visualization. Be a fucking magician who creates his ideal life.

Thought forms come to life in the ether, an egregore is created and it brings you what you ask for.

Believe me the fucking power is real.

Mandamme Blatasky was right.

Redheads, the vampire's favorite girls.

It is necessary to pay attention because the external aspect of the woman denotes what her interior is like. So a redhead girl, a girl with fire-colored hair, is just that, fire, a very hot girl. They are usually very white skinned girls, super well made, who have a perfect face, a perfect body, very big tits, very big ass and an elastic, white and rubbery flesh that is very pleasurable, and is excellent for what we like most, passionate sex.

Therefore, they will always be superior, they will always be the ones chosen by the seductive vampire, an expert of love who has tested hundreds of women, and in the end he really knows what he wants, which is a beautiful redhead ass, to fuck her until dawn. And if he can enslave her sexually, so much the better. This is what the seductive vampire wants.

The life of the seductive vampire.

The seductive vampire is an enthusiast of life, likes to enjoy, go out, stay up late, seduce, do crazy and sometimes even dangerous things. They love to travel to exotic places. Enjoyment happens in every moment, it is not only what happens to you or what you do, but how you are enjoying what is happening to you.

I think there is no one happier and more carefree than a seductive vampire whose only goal is to enjoy himself. You really live life without worrying about nonsense and being happy no matter what happens to you. Besides, as you always think good things, good things happen to you and so, believing yourself exempt from suffering any evil, this materializes and you live a wonderful life, where everything good imagined, and more, appears as if by magic in the life of the seductive vampire. Nothing can take the smile off the vampire seducer's face. People can't even imagine what it feels like when you are fulfilling your predatory function.

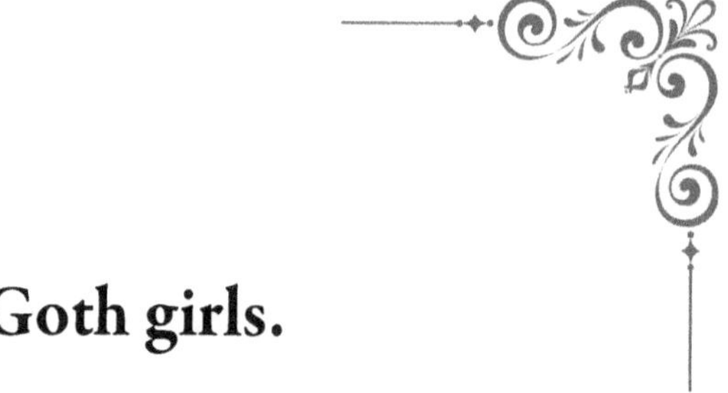

Goth girls.

These girls are clearly different from vampires in that they are girls who do not go around hunting as vampires do, but simply have a very cool aesthetic and are beautiful and attractive to the seducer. Quite the opposite of a vampire girl who thinks she's the best, is quite stuck up and does practically what the vampire does, but without any merit, because it's very easy to let herself score goals and very difficult to score them. Gothic girls listen to Marilyn Manson and Rammstein, they paint their lips black, wear black clothes, lace, painted nails and shaved pussies and why not say it? they are very hot and morbid. So except for the vampire girls who are also gothic girls, but they are assholes, these other more normal girls who simply dress like this, are recommendable to incorporate into the life of the seductive vampire.

Motorcycles and risk.

The seductive vampire is quite oblivious and reckless and has a taste for speed, but must control himself for his own good. He likes fast motorcycles and badass cars. It is with motorcycles where the seductive vampire shows more manliness, and where he plays the most, putting them at high speeds. I recommend to have black motorcycles and ride them rather slowly, custom motorcycles, harley type, to ride quietly seeing and being seen, without the need to run like a madman that we are not in a race.

A tough, good-looking guy is riding down the road with his motorcycle, leather jacket, and sunglasses. He stops at the bar, has a few beers, and then on the way out of the bar he continues, but this time with a pretty girl he just met sitting on the back of the bike.

Reading minds.

Yes, the vampire seducer is a telepath, a mentalist, a person who understands the thoughts of others because he knows how to read body language perfectly, and knows when they like, when they dislike, when they are happy, when they are sad, when they are pretending, and what they are really thinking.

All this information is then used to unmask them, tell them the truth, surprise them with your in-depth knowledge of them, and hallucinate them. You get into their minds and anticipate their moves. This is learned with hundreds of years dedicated to seduction, and also with vampiric powers that allow you to see inside their brain, and know what they want and why. Yes, we vampire seducers read our women's minds, and we know how to get them to do what we want. We have developed "the detector" that tells us everything they are thinking instantly.

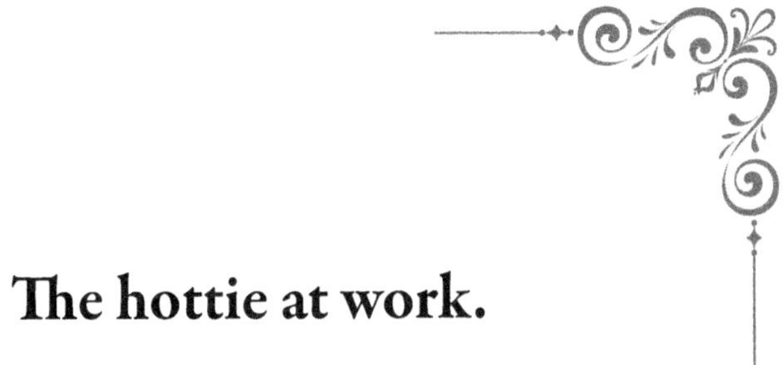

The hottie at work.

It's not that it's advisable, it's your fucking obligation, to hook up with that hottie from work that you see every day, and because of constantly seeing her, you're mortified that you're not still enjoying her gorgeous body.

These are the first ones that the vampire seducer must flirt with, because as the psychopath of "the silence of the lambs" said, we want what we see, and if we see this one, we want this one. These so desired triumphs are worth much more than the normal ones, so if you want to be a good vampire seducer start flirting with this one and make a name for yourself in your office as a flirt.

Be careful if the thing ends badly and she becomes your enemy. It will mortify you too, so try to pick her up and let her stay, or at least if you let her finish the thing satisfactorily, and you end up cold hard and completely independent, because if you still like her you will be very screwed and you will not be a real seducer, a real seducer does not suffer with his exes.

The car of the seductive vampire.

Almost all of us would like to have a sports car or at least a high-end car, but I tell you one thing, it is not necessary so much ostentation to be happy, nor to attract girls, just having a normal car that you like is enough. We please ourselves by having the car we fucking like and if they don't like it, they can go fuck themselves. Let them buy it and then we get in it, and while we're at it we criticize like they do.

Refined manners.

The seductive vampire is a dandy who is very elegantly dressed, has an impressive culture, but really impressive, elegant bearing and fine gestures, elegance and distinction. This is not the same as the charming scoundrel who goes anyway and does not care what people think of him. The seductive vampire is refined, polite, courteous and sybaritic.

He does not eat just anything, only seafood, tasty fish, fruits and vegetables, leaving meat for rare occasions, as he considers it a bit primitive to eat meat. The seductive vampire will delight in listening to classical music and will have an extensive music collection. The seductive vampire will have his house super clean and tidy and will invite his girlfriends over to listen to him play the organ. He plays the musical organ and also the other organ, the sexual organ, which they like to be played more than the musical one.

The vampire seducer is a brilliant composer, a scholar, a sage, women appreciate and value all that inner world, and baggage and extensive experience. The vampire seducer was already said decades ago that he had had 40 lives, well now 80! and so he continues adding lives, experiences, anecdotes that others could not even imagine.

The girl who goes with the vampire seducer is amazed by his finesse and elegance, and therefore attracted by these unusual qualities. The seductive vampire clearly belongs to the school of poise and is in great demand by the local girls.

The fragrant and shady forest.

In the cold starry night the crazy seducer vampire goes to a dark forest, but scary and scary and there he does his meditations and his madness. You have to put some really big eggs, but the vampire seducer sets goals of self-improvement and this is one of them. Going alone to the forest at night and being there for a long time, what a thing to do! Well, that's what a vampire seducer does to overcome his fears.

Sometimes you hear sounds that sound like voices produced by the wind, noises, birds chirping, anything is scary, but there is the seductive vampire holding the pressure like a male. Because he is a man and a man can do anything he sets his mind to.

The triad.

Again the triad, again the fucking triad. We have already talked so much about it that I don't have much to tell, but I will tell you something important, that you don't have to look for it, that you don't encourage this to form. Any attempt to look more formal will not work, it is just like that, crazy and fucker as they prefer you, and they will be the ones who will come to you while you are totally passive and independent of them. And it won't be a triad, it will be much more.

The one who goes around trying to get their loyalty to have them fails, you have to be totally cold and detached and very funny and they themselves are the ones who will want to be there in the triad.

I have called it a triad to put something minimal, normally sets of many women are formed, in the most extreme case, in which I was in danger of death by so much madness and fornication, I got to make an octet. Remember that the more you have, the more they come to you, to the point that you will not be able to go on and you will fall ill from so much physical exhaustion.

Culture and art.

The seductive vampire goes to the theater, to the opera, to the classical music concert, to the lecture on the romantic writers of the nineteenth century, to every cultural event that interests him, to every concert, exhibition of paintings, art museum that attracts him. To every cathedral or mosque, to every ruin, to every castle, to every palace. Everything related to art and culture is of enormous interest to him.

He reads books in English, books about the Romans and their architecture, about buildings, skyscrapers, science, antiquity. The seductive vampire likes art and will have objects such as paintings or tapestries, or any artistic representation that pleases him.

The seductive vampire is a musical composer, he also makes handicrafts, treasures numerous precious stones that he looks at and draws his energy from them as well, as well as crystal balls and other objects considered sacred to him.

The seductive vampire is also a painter and thus expresses his inner world.

The seductive vampire writes numerous books, essays, and novels on all subjects that interest him.

The seductive vampire researches and delves into every subject that is worthy of his attention, and in many of them he specializes and becomes an expert.

The seductive vampire learns other languages, travels and learns every day of his life.

The vampire seducer's goal is to maximize his knowledge and joyful experiences, especially with attractive girls.

The seductive vampire will attend gatherings and will be a brilliant speaker at such meetings.

The seductive vampire is just that, a wise, charismatic man who enraptures people with his wonderful ability to involve them in his projects and motivate them to achieve their goals.

The seductive vampire is also a life coach who shows by example what life should be like, and also helps people very selflessly to improve their lives.

The vampire seducer is a man put here to help others and get them to give the best version of themselves.

The seductive vampire is a guide.

Pub.

The place where the vampire gets 90% of his triumphs, that dark place, full of people, atmosphere and music, where everything is possible and magic happens. It is extremely important for your performance as a flirt that the place where you go pleases you and excites you. It is really very difficult to flirt when you are in a pub where you don't like the atmosphere, you don't like the people, you don't like the music, you don't like the decoration, you don't like anything. You don't feel comfortable, it's practically impossible, that's why it's very important that you find your magic place, your cove, your special place where you feel great. This place has to have an appropriate market for you, for example if you are 40 years old, it has to be a place where 40 year old people go, not 19 year old people. You have to like the music, you have to like the decoration, you have to like the philosophy of the place.

I believe that one of the most important issues to succeed in seduction is to find that great place where you feel comfortable and happy, once you are there you start to materialize your power, to obtain triumphs, to gain confidence, to have positive memories of that same place, and it becomes a fetish place, just knowing that you are there and you feel powerful.

In Santiago I had my fishing ground in the 90's and 2000 until let's say the decade of the ten where the environment changed, this fishing ground was "la Quintana" a tremendous pub where everything was possible. There was also "el retablo" quite close to the yields of this one, but it was the Quintana the one I liked the most. Once I was there euphoric I said

This is the Quintana!

Like the Spartan in 300.

There I felt strong and powerful and it showed. Nowadays, due to the extreme age I have reached, it is no longer my fetish place because the environment has totally changed and people are 30 years younger than me. The important thing is that it existed. And there will also be other new places where it will be great. Find your place!

The colors of the vampire.

The vampire is a fan of red and black which are the two colors he likes the most. They are in the cape and they are in many parts of the vampire. Notice a lot of women wearing red, women wearing red are hot women, especially if they are wearing red shoes. These red shoes give away their horny mind. I know this from decades of experience in noticing how they are dressed and what they look like. The more red they wear, the more acts they are to throw at you.

Red denotes power, passion, fire, strength, security. Dress in red too, you will not go unnoticed. Black will give you mystery and elegance.

Notice women who wear red lips as well, anything that they wear red is a good sign.

Vampiric fetishisms.

It is not the vampire's fault that he has become a fetishist, it is they who have perverted you with their multiple follies. So finally at the age of 40 the vampire ends up becoming a fetishist who likes colorful toe nails. You like to suck and eat them and it's very exciting. This as I said is their fault, their perversions, before starting to fuck en masse I was a totally normal guy, now that they have driven you half crazy if one of them doesn't put her toes painted red in your mouth you are not happy at all. The truth is that this is a delicacy, a delicacy as rich as pussy or tits. Yes, be a perverted sybarite and do these things that give so much morbid. A vampire is also a fetishist, a moderate fetishist who doesn't reach Tarantino's levels of crazy, but a little fetishist yes.

Vampire genre.

Now that one can feel like a woman and be a woman, or feel like a giraffe and be a giraffe, why shouldn't I feel like a vampire and be a vampire? Well, I'm going to go to the civil registry to see if they will let me put my vampire gender on it and thus make my vampirism official, and when they ask me if I'm a man I will say no, that I'm a vampire, and by the way I will pass through the feminist laws that criminalize men. As I will not be a man but a vampire they will not affect me ha ha ha ha ha ha. Let's take advantage of the bullshit that progressives do for our benefit.

Hunting.

The vampire is already in his natural environment, the pub. He has gone out alone, there he is positioned carefully observing the girls of the place. Suddenly one of them catches his attention, it is a blonde girl in a white dress with excellent curves. This girl is at the bar alone, because she has gone to order her drink there. The vampire's detector has validated her as optimal to be approached. She is really a magnificent piece, she has very good thighs, very good type, very attractive, very beautiful. The vampire looks at her from afar, she looks at him, he smiles slightly and she lowers her gaze a little embarrassed as she has realized that the vampire knows she was looking at him, this is just the sign she needed. The vampire doesn't hesitate even for a moment, it's been only two seconds since he realized that the girl was there and he's already going to approach her totally determined. The vampire takes advantage of the strategic situation and the enormous opportunity offered by the fact that she is alone. The vampire stands next to her, smiles and says.

-They are taking longer and longer to attend.

She laughs and replies

-I've been here for a while now and no one is coming.

-I'll get it for you.

Says the vampire confidently and calls the waiter who in a short time appears to

Meanwhile the vampire has already introduced himself and given two kisses, the girl's name is Alicia for example, she is from out of town and is here and passing through with some friends going out tonight, soon she will go to her city which for example could be Valladolid.

The vampire has more data than he needs, he knows what he has to do, the vampire has realized that she is a pretty girl who is out having a good time out of town, which makes her much more uninhibited, she doesn't know the place very well, and she is receptive to talk, so the vampire will set his predation in motion immediately.

The vampire asks

- who are you with?

and she replies

-With some friends from here in Santiago- -With some friends from here in Santiago-.

The vampire says

- I am the most knowledgeable person in this city and I can take you to the best places.

so he is giving her an advantage, a benefit, he is being kind, he is being polite, plus she sees that he is alone and after how well he has liked her it would be a bit unpleasant not to give him a part in the evening and leave him out.

Where are your friends? Come on, I want to meet them.

The vampire goes with Alice and introduces himself to her three other friends, of course much uglier than this one. He will be polite, courteous, gentlemanly and nice to them so that they feel comfortable. He is there telling things, being funny, the girls are comfortable and little by little an atmosphere of warmth and well-being is established between him and them. They have totally accepted him. Now after about 20 minutes the vampire offers to take them on a tour of the city to the coolest pubs. Although they are from Santiago they always go to the same place and they don't know how the vampire who has been dedicated to the night for 30 years. The vampire takes them to another darker and more propitious pub, one with more music, with more people, where everyone is closer and this intrusion in the personal barriers makes them accept him even more because he and Alicia's friends are practically touching each other.

In this pub he will begin to create comfort and a slight complicity with looks and smiles with Alicia, she is comfortable and begins to lightly touch her hair. The vampire doesn't tell her how beautiful she is, or give her compliments, or anything, he's just there emanating masculinity, being fun, uninhibited, very unconcerned about flirting with her. He's just having fun and they are having fun with him. You can tell he's comfortable, he's not afraid of them, he's used to going with girls.

Some of her friends are attracted to him and start hitting on him a lot and asking him questions, this is a great sign, because it means that he is attracting women and doing things right. Incidentally the vampire is now concentrating on this girl and this makes Alicia feel a bit abandoned, she realizes more that she wants to be with him and have more prominence. the vampire disguising his conversation with the other friend of education is making her suffer.

Then they all drink more alcohol and laugh. When Alice feels abandoned, the vampire says to her

-I'll show you the best of this place.

you take her by the hand for example and lead her to a more secluded place where you tell her -

the best thing about this site is me

Once you have separated her from her friends, she feels more comfortable and she gets closer and touches you a lot, your head goes and you start to grab her by the waist and do not let go, you feel very comfortable and comfortable with her and you feel a very strong attraction as a result of this minimum space between friends and the high physical contact you are having. You make a rogue face, you are uninhibited and in this case shameless and you touch her hair a little bit, and wow! Without further ado you go over and kiss her there. This place is often the bar of the pub and to reward you for this good kiss you order yourself a cubata that tastes like glory.

Then you're making out hard with this girl and the second you snog or grab one of her buttocks from her ass and knead it hard to finish you tell her -what an ass you have-.

Alicia sticks her tongue further into your mouth and then you tell her

-I want you to come and sleep with me.

Alicia answers

-I'm with my friends.

and you answer

-Don't worry, I don't eat anyone, besides, when you want to come back I'll take you back.

This sentence and another stronger snog that follows totally convince Alicia and she goes with the vampire to see her friends and tells them that she is going with you.

You leave the pub and on the way you give him three or four more snogs, get to the car, get in it and get home.

There without much ado you lie down on the bed and you can imagine what happens. The vampire spends the night fucking wonderfully this unknown and lustful woman he has just met.

The vampire fucks her on all fours, on top of her, she on top of him, she sucks him off, and you cum three times in her wet, hot pussy.

In the morning when you wake up, you think, and I was going to lose everything by not approaching her! God, how many women are lost by being a coward.

But not you, the vampire, you are no coward and you have proved it.

When Alicia wakes up in the morning, having slept very little, you take her to her friends and go home happy and satisfied with the duty accomplished.

You write down in the list the new piece you have achieved and you sleep pleasantly. When you wake up then you realize the wonders you have enjoyed and you get the rush, you acquire more self-concept, more self-esteem, more fucking power.

You feel like the fucking master, the boss of the city, the fucking master and that's how it is.

And this is the hunt, this is what makes us seducers, vampires and all of God live. Long live the hunt.

The girl, what difference does it make! She will be back and by the time you want to call her, a month will have passed and the moment will be lost. That girl will never be lost, she will remain forever part of your power. It helps to be aware of your fucking power. Great girl. That one brings more than any girlfriend.

That girl made you feel like a macho, a fucker, a fucking winner. She didn't make trouble, she just brought it. The best of your life.

The vampire speaks to you.

You who are reading or listening to this, wherever you are and whoever you are, you are my friend. I identify with you and your problems, because I have gone through all of them and I have suffered as the most, and thanks to go through many hardships of all kinds, economic, sexual, loving, emotional, thanks to go through crisis and above all thanks to the immense work and huge effort to move forward and not give up and try to improve, without settling for what you are, I have reached where I am.

I want you to go as high as you want to go, because there really are no limits, but you settle for something you take for granted. I want you to understand that I would like to influence you in a more powerful way than through this book, and in fact I will make videos where everything will be better explained I hope, but for now this is what there is, and you must take advantage of it well and motivate yourself well to transform yourself into what you want to be.

Now from the wisdom that comes with age I see all the past clearly and I am very proud of what I have done and excited to do new things. I am the vampire, the vampire fucker who terrorized this city for decades, and I am handing over to you to carry on my legacy in your city, being a fun loving vampire fucker who lives a wonderful life.

I don't want this! I want this! I want that! I'm going to fight for this! Be irreverent and don't stop until you reach your goal.

Be the impaler.

The dark one.

The dreaded.

The most powerful.

Be a fucking vampire seducer.

The triumph must not only be with women, it must be holistic, it must be total.

Men need to wake up and realize that the life of the seductive vampire is far more satisfying than any other.

While people wake up, we who already know what we are, continue our predation.

I know everything, I see everything, I know what you think, I see your aura even from a distance, I am the vampire.

This is what I have to tell of the seductive vampire. Thank you for listening to me.

The night of the vampire.

Yes, tonight is the best night of your life, tonight you will go out in the gloomy alleys of your city. Make sure it's dark, night is our friend. Yes, today you are going out to seduce a gorgeous gothic girl that you will meet in a dark and tumultuous pub. Then at dawn if the conquest was good you return to your abode to hide from the sun with her, Take advantage of this night with her, it's what you have, live the moment. Vampires live like that, from moment to moment.

The best night of your life,

Translated with DeepL.com (free version)

Let's play!

Did you love *The Vampire Seducer*? Then you should read *Attract Women with Masculinity*[1] by John Danen!

[2]

Learn the art of attracting women with masculinity. Transmit your most masculine qualities and become a man coveted by women.

---

1. https://books2read.com/u/mKdnAL

2. https://books2read.com/u/mKdnAL

Also by John Danen

Seduction 5.0
S.A.X.
Chicas complicadas
Seducción 5.0
El libro del tonto
Macho Alpha
Macho alpha extracto
La seducción después de la pandemia
Terriblemente atractivo
Seducción 5.1
Sedução 5.1
How to be Cool and Attractive
Sedução. Avançada. X.
Garotas complicadas
¡Basta de ser buen chico! Sé un chico malo.
El método JD. El método de seducción de John Danen
El arte de agradarte a ti mismo
¡Basta ya de abusos! ¡Defiéndete!
Enought with the abuse! Defend yourself!
Máster en seducción
Las mujeres. El amor. Y el sexo.
Supera la dependencia emocional
Atrae mujeres con masculinidad
JD Absoluta seducción
El fracaso del amor

Entender a las mujeres

La vida del seductor sinvergüenza y encantador.

El arte de la dureza

Terrivelmente atraente

Deixe de ser um bom da fita! Seja um mauzão.

Superar a dependência emocional

A arte de se agradar

Pare o abuso! Defenda-se!

O fracasso do amor.

O método JD

Don´t Be a Good Boy! Be a Badass

Complicated girls

The Art of Pleasing Yourself

Duro y Sinvergüenza

Mestre en sedução

JD Method

The Failure of Love. The Trap of Serious Relationships

Master in Seduction

A. S. X. Advanced. Seduction. X

Women. Love. Sex

How to Become a Real Man. Be an Alpha Male

Attract Women with Masculinity

JD Absolut Seductión

Understanding Women

The Life of the Shameless and Charming Seducer.

The Art of Toughness

Tough and Shameless

Überwindung der Emotionalen Abhängigkeit

Maître en séduction

Schrecklich Attraktiv

Surmonter la Dépendance Émotionnelle

L'art de la dureté

Die Kunst der Zähigkeit

Hör auf, ein guter Junge zu sein, sei ein böser Junge

Assez D'être un Bon Garçon ! Sois un Mauvais Garçon.

Die Kunst, sich Selbst zu Gefallen

Dur et sans Vergogne

Hart im Nehmen und Schamlos

L'art de se Plaire à soi-Même

Das Scheitern der Liebe

L'échec de L'amour.

Meister der Verführung

Die JD-Methode

Maestro di Seduzione

Terriblement Attrayant

La Méthode JD

Capire le donne

Compreendendo as Mulheres

Comprendre les Femmes

Die Frauen Verstehen

Les Filles Compliquées

Komplizierte Mädchen

JD Séduction Absolue

La Vie du Séducteur Charmant et sans Vergogne

Les Femmes. L'amour. Et le Sexe.

Mâle Alpha

S.A.X.

V.F.X.

Donne. Amore. E il sesso.

Ragazze Complicate

Superare la Dipendenza Emotiva

Seduzione. Avanzata. X.

Dark Seducción

Il Fallimento Dell'amore.

Il Metodo JD

Alphamännchen

Atrair Mulheres com Masculinidade
Attirare le donne con la Mascolinità
Attirer les Femmes par la Masculinité
Mit Männlichkeit Frauen Anziehen
Frauen. Liebe. Und Sex.
L'arte di Piacere a se Stessi
Mulheres. Amor. E Sexo.
JD Seduzione Assoluta
JD Absolute Verführung
JD Sedução Absoluta
Das Leben des charmanten, schamlosen Verführers
Smettila di Fare il Bravo Ragazzo! Essere un Cattivo Ragazzo.
La Vita del Seduttore Affascinante e Spudorato
A Vida do Sedutor Encantador e sem Vergonha
Macho Alfa
Uomo Alfa
Séduction 5.0
Verführung 5.0
Seduzione 5.0
Duro e Senza Vergogna
Duro e Sem Vergonha
L'arte della Durezza
A Arte da Dureza
The Fool's Book
Das Buch der Dummköpfe
Il Libro dei Pazzi
O Livro do Tolo
Dark Seduction
Dunkle Verführung
Sedução Escura
Dark Seduction
Seduzione Oscura
Le livre du fou

Como materializar lo que deseas con el fxxxxxx power
Como materializar o que você quer com o Fxxxxxx Power
El ángel Sex-terminador
El seductor vampiro
O Vampiro Sedutor
Sex-Terminating Angel
The Vampire Seducer
How to Materialize What You Want With The Fxxxxxx Power
El camino del maestro
Il vampiro seduttore
O camiño do mestre
La via del maestro
Der verführerische Vampir
Le sedusant vampire
Der Weg des Meisters
La voie du maître de la séduction
The Way of the Master
Come materializzare ciò che si desidera con il Fxxxxxx Power
Wie Sie Ihre Wünsche verwirklichen können mit dem Fxxxxxx Power
El método EDP
O método EDP
The EDP method

About the Author

Español.

Soy un hombre vividor y divertido que busca el lado bueno de las cosas siempre.

Mi experiencia es el campo de las relaciones personales y de la seducción. Por eso tras dedicarme larguísimas décadas a ello, quiero trasmitir mis conocimientos. Para que las nuevas generaciones tengan unos conceptos que les den una ventaja competitiva sostenible y poderosa en el campo del amor.

Quiero ayudarte a a conseguir tus metas.

Portugués.

Sou um homem animado, e divertido, que sempre procura o lado bom das coisas.

Minha experiência está no campo das relações pessoais e da sedução. É por isso que, após décadas de dedicação a ela, quero transmitir meus conhecimentos.

Quero ajudá-los a alcançar seus objetivos.

Inglés

I am a lively and fun man, who always looks for the good side of things.

My experience is in the field of personal relationships and seduction. That is why, after decades of dedicating myself to it, I want to pass on my knowledge. So that the new generations have concepts that give them a sustainable and powerful competitive advantage in the field of love.

I want to help you achieve your goals

Français Je suis un homme vif et drôle qui cherche toujours le bon côté des choses.

Mon expérience se situe dans le domaine des relations personnelles et de la séduction. C'est pourquoi, après m'y être consacré pendant des décennies, je veux transmettre mes connaissances. Pour que les nouvelles générations disposent de concepts qui leur donnent un avantage concurrentiel durable et puissant dans le domaine de l'amour.

Je veux vous aider à atteindre vos objectifs.